Doctor Potty
by Hadas Kaplan

Written by: Hadas Kaplan

Illustrated by: Mark Niño Balita

Edited by: Ayelet Tsabari, Trisha Alcisto

Translated by: Grace Michaeli

Design & Art Direction by: ZIS | Targeted Design

Copyright © 2018 by Hadas Kaplan
All rights reserved. No part of this publication may be reproduced, distributed, or transmitted in any form or by any means, including photocopying, recording, or other electronic or mechanical methods, without the prior written permission of the publisher.
Printed in the United States of America

DOCTOR POTTY

Written by: Hadas Kaplan

Illustrated by: Mark Niño Balita

This is Tommy.
His real name is Thomas, but everyone calls him Tommy.

Tommy likes playing with blocks, reading stories, and pretending to be an animal doctor.

One day, Tommy's mommy and daddy learned that even small children can use the potty, and they agreed that Tommy would feel much better without a diaper.

Before bedtime, Daddy read Tommy one of his favorite books, a story about a doctor who helps animals.

When they finished the story, Daddy patted Tommy's head and said, "You know, buddy, tomorrow you will be wearing underwear! Just like Mommy, Daddy, and… the animal doctor!"

Tommy smiled and mumbled, "Doctor," and then he closed his eyes and fell asleep.

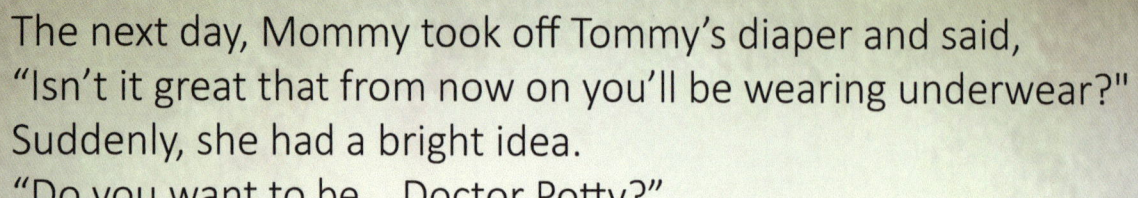

The next day, Mommy took off Tommy's diaper and said, "Isn't it great that from now on you'll be wearing underwear?" Suddenly, she had a bright idea.
"Do you want to be... Doctor Potty?"
Tommy's eyes shone.

Mommy said, "Which underwear would you like to wear? The ones with the stars? Or the ones with the bears?"

Tommy pointed to the underwear with the bears, waved his hands in the air, and shouted, "Doctor Potty!"

"I want to show you something," Mommy said,
taking Tommy to the bathroom.
"This is your potty. You can pee and poop in it,
just like Mommy and Daddy!"

Tommy said, "Poop!"
And put the potty on his head.

Sometimes Tommy peed on the floor. And Mommy would say, "Doctor Potty, we pee in the potty."

Sometimes Tommy peed on his toys.

And Daddy would say, "Doctor Potty, we pee in the potty."

Mommy and Daddy took Tommy to the potty many times.

Sometimes he sat there and read his book about the animals and the doctor.

Sometimes he played with his princess stickers.

And sometimes Tommy didn't want to go to the potty. Sometimes, he was too busy!
Doctor Potty had to make important things with his Legos, or build tall buildings, or put his dolls to sleep.
It's not like you can just stop doing those things whenever you want to!

Once, when Tommy was busy, Mommy said, "Do you want to go to the potty like a roaring lion or a hopping bunny?"
Tommy put his toy aside and hopped with Mommy to the bathroom.

And sometimes... Sometimes he peed in the potty!

Mommy beamed. "You peed! Inside your potty!"
Daddy said, "What a good aim, Tommy! I mean, Doctor Potty!"

Daddy picked Tommy up and swirled him around, saying:
"Doctor Potty used the potty!" and Tommy laughed and squealed.

The days passed, and Doctor Potty—Tommy, that is—
peed and pooped, sometimes in his potty,
and sometimes in his underwear.

Mommy and Daddy kept taking him to the bathroom and saying, "Doctor Potty, we pee in the potty."

Until one day, Tommy came to Mommy and Daddy and said: "Daddy! Mommy! Pee-pee!"

Daddy looked everywhere for the puddle of pee.
But he couldn't find it.

Mommy said, "I'm going to check if there's a puddle in the playroom!" But Mommy couldn't find a puddle anywhere.

"I know!" said Daddy, "Maybe there's a puddle in the living room."

But Daddy couldn't find a puddle there, either.

Mommy was a bit confused.
Then, she noticed Tommy's underwear was dry.
Suddenly, she had an idea!
"Pee-pee? Do you have to go pee?" she asked hesitantly.

Tommy smiled and nodded: "Yes! Pee-pee!"
Daddy smiled and said, "It's great that you came to us, Doctor!"

Quickly, let's run to the bathroom!"
And they all ran to bathroom, Mommy, Daddy, and Tommy—
that is, Doctor Potty.

Mommy helped Tommy take off his underwear.
Tommy looked, aimed, and... peed! Right inside the potty!
"Great shot!" Mommy exclaimed. And Daddy smiled.

After Tommy finished and washed his hands, they all danced the "Doctor peed in the potty" dance, but because the bathroom was too small to dance, they moved to the living room.

"Doctor Potty used the potty!" Daddy exclaimed loudly.

And since then, whenever Tommy is awake, he wears underwear, sometimes with cars, sometimes with stars, and sometimes with hearts.
Mommy said she will look for underwear with animals, just like the animals in his book.

Mommy and Daddy take Tommy to the bathroom, and sometimes Tommy even tells them he has to pee. Then, they all go together, and they never forget to dance the "Doctor Potty peed in the potty" dance.